PENGUIN B(

THAT'S QUITE A DRESS
YOU ALMOST HAVE ON

Craig Bennett is an entertainment reporter and has written for a variety of publications including the *Daily Mirror* and *Daily Telegraph*. He is a regular on television and can be heard on radio across Australia and New Zealand dishing out the latest Tinseltown news. Craig lived in Hollywood from 1999 to 2001 and reported on everything from the Oscars to Elizabeth Taylor's newest health crisis and the contents of Pamela Anderson's handbag. He now lives in Sydney with his pet pythons.

THAT'S quite a Dress you ALMOST HAVE on

CRAIG BENNETT

PENGUIN BOOKS

PENGUIN BOOKS

Published by the Penguin Group
Penguin Group (Australia)
250 Camberwell Road, Camberwell, Victoria 3124, Australia
(a division of Pearson Australia Group Pty Ltd)
Penguin Group (USA) Inc.
375 Hudson Street, New York, New York 10014, USA
Penguin Group (Canada)
90 Eglinton Avenue East, Suite 700, Toronto, Canada ON M4P 2Y3
(a division of Pearson Penguin Canada Inc.)
Penguin Books Ltd
80 Strand, London WC2R 0RL England
Penguin Ireland
25 St Stephen's Green, Dublin 2, Ireland
(a division of Penguin Books Ltd)
Penguin Books India Pvt Ltd
11 Community Centre, Panchsheel Park, New Delhi – 110 017, India
Penguin Group (NZ)
67 Apollo Drive, Rosedale, North Shore 0632, New Zealand
(a division of Pearson New Zealand Ltd)
Penguin Books (South Africa) (Pty) Ltd
24 Sturdee Avenue, Rosebank, Johannesburg 2196, South Africa

Penguin Books Ltd, Registered Offices: 80 Strand, London, WC2R 0RL, England

First published by Penguin Group (Australia), 2007

1 3 5 7 9 10 8 6 4 2

Text copyright © Craig Bennett 2007

The moral right of the author has been asserted

Cover and text design by Elizabeth Dias © Penguin Group (Australia)
Cover illustration by Brian Clinton
Author photograph by David Hahn
Internal illustrations from CSA Images
Typeset by Post Pre-press Group, Brisbane, Queensland
Printed and bound in Australia by McPherson's Printing Group, Maryborough, Victoria

National Library of Australia
Cataloguing-in-Publication data:

Bennett, Craig, 1962–
That's quite a dress you almost have on.
Bibliography.
Includes index.
ISBN 978 0 14 300672 5.
1. Motion pictures – Quotations, maxims, etc. 2. Invective.
I. Title.

791.430207

penguin.com.au

CONTENTS

INTRODUCTION

My life has been a constant blur of showbiz, celebrities and movies.

As an entertainment reporter interviewing the stars and dishing out the latest Hollywood gossip, I know movies. I've always been fascinated by the nasty, scathing, ultra-camp lines – those bitchy barbs and backhanders that underscore the drama, the mayhem and the tension of what's happening on screen.

Ever since the first talkie flickered to life, the movies have churned out an array of crackling comebacks, witty one-liners, waspy wisecracks, lusty lampoons, poisonous punchlines, withering witticisms, racy rejoinders, raunchy retorts, sarcastic sideswipes, bitchy backhanders, insidious insults, punch-in-the-mouth putdowns and caustic quips.

And it's the sassy, saucy, sexy style with which those acidic lines are delivered that makes you want to stand up and applaud wildly, while wishing those bon mots had been rolling from your lips.

For me, it all began with Bette Davis' immortal line in **All About Eve**: 'Fasten your seatbelts, it's going to be a bumpy night!' The line, and the film, captured my ten-year-old imagination. I was spellbound.

How often have *you* heard a killer line of dialogue and thought 'I wish I'd said that'? Well, now you can. Enjoy!

QUOTES

'Paris is for lovers. Maybe
that's why I stayed only
thirty-five minutes.'

Linus Larrabee, *played by*
HUMPHREY BOGART *in* **Sabrina** (1954)

\/ \/ \/ \/

'If you look at her carefully,
there are so many lines on
her face you could drive a
train on it.'

Marina Rudd, *played by* ELIZABETH TAYLOR
in **The Mirror Crack'd** (1980)

'I'd like to ask you to stay and have a drink, but I'm afraid you might accept.'

Lynn Markham, *played by* JOAN CRAWFORD *in* **Female On The Beach** (1955)

III

'I'd like to take you south of my border and north of my garter.'

Marguerita Ventura, *played by* LAINIE KAZAN *in* **Lust In The Dust** (1985)

III

'You have exactly ten seconds to change that look of disgusting pity into one of enormous respect.'

Max Bialystock, *played by* ZERO MOSTEL *in* **The Producers** (1968)

3

'I don't use a pen. I write with a goose quill dipped in venom.'

Waldo Lydecker, *played by* **CLIFTON WEBB** *in* **Laura** (1944)

////

'She'll sting you one day. Oh, ever so gently so you hardly even feel it. Until you fall down dead.'

Jennifer Stewart, *played by* **LUCY MARLOW** *in* **Queen Bee** (1955)

'A girl's best friend is a good, loopin' right [hook].'

Pearl White, *played by* BETTY HUTTON *in* **The Perils Of Pauline** (1947)

////

'I hate to tell you, dear, but your skin makes the Rocky Mountains look like chiffon velvet.'

Mrs Spencer's friend, *played by* LENITA LANE *in* **The Women** (1939)

////

'The screwing I'm getting isn't worth the screwing I'm getting.'

Gwen, *played by* FAYE DUNAWAY *in* **The Arrangement** (1969)

'Chewing gum helps me think.'
'Sweetie, you're wasting your gum.'

Celsius, *played by* LUCA TOMMASSINI, *to* Albert Goldman, *played by* NATHAN LANE *in* **The Birdcage** (1996)

////

'Did you eat something sour for lunch today?'

Bill, *played by* WILLIAM CORSON *in* **Stage Door** (1937)

////

'Roll up your mouth, you talk too much. If I'd have known how much you talk I would never have come out of my coma.'

Sir Wilfrid Robarts, *played by* CHARLES LAUGHTON *in* **Witness For The Prosecution** (1957)

'I know your type. I know a slap from a slug.'

Amanda Bonner, *played by* KATHARINE HEPBURN *in* **Adam's Rib** (1949)

////

'I'm nobody's fool, least of all yours.'

Addison DeWitt, *played by* GEORGE SANDERS *in* **All About Eve** (1950)

////

'A cat's a better mother than you.'

Rhett Butler, *played by* CLARK GABLE *in* **Gone With The Wind** (1939)

7

'Children would only get in the way of our erotic lifestyle.'

Sandra Sullivan, *played by* MINK STOLE *in* **Polyester** (1981)

/ / / /

'Stop wearing out that mirror.'

Marion, *played by* SARAH CHADWICK *in* **The Adventures Of Priscilla, Queen Of The Desert** (1994)

/ / / /

'You're as funny as a cry for help.'

The Tiny Waitress, *played by* JODY GILBERT *in* **Never Give A Sucker An Even Break** (1941)

'I'd rather swallow razor blades than have a drink with you.'

Rhonda Epinstalk, *played by* RACHEL GRIFFITHS *in* **Muriel's Wedding** (1994)

////

'This is not an affair, it's a one-night stand that happened twice.'

Detective Leon Zat, *played by* ANTHONY LAPAGLIA *in* **Lantana** (2001)

'Take your clammy hands off my chair. You have the touch of a love-starved cobra.'

Sheridan Whiteside, *played by* MONTY WOOLLEY *in* **The Man Who Came To Dinner** (1942)

////

'Maybe I left my sense of humour in my other suit.'

Sidney Falco, *played by* TONY CURTIS *in* **Sweet Smell Of Success** (1957)

////

'What's a dazzling urbanite like you doing in a rustic setting like this?'

Jim, the Waco Kid, *played by* GENE WILDER *in* **Blazing Saddles** (1974)

'I've told you a million times not to talk to me when I'm doing my lashes.'

Kitty Packard, *played by* JEAN HARLOW *in* **Dinner At Eight** (1933)

░░░░

'He was to the bottle what Louis Armstrong was to the trumpet.'

Nasser, *played by* SAEED JAFFREY *in* **My Beautiful Laundrette** (1985)

'Ladies, you have to be strong and independent, and remember, don't get mad, get everything!'

IVANA TRUMP, *playing herself in* **The First Wives Club** (1996)

////

'Where's your decency? In what rubbish dump?'

Millicent Wetherby, *played by* JOAN CRAWFORD *in* **Autumn Leaves** (1956)

'I'd like to kiss you, but I've just washed my hair.'

Madge Norwood, *played by* BETTE DAVIS *in* **The Cabin In The Cotton**
(1932)

////

'You are physically repulsive, intellectually retarded,
you're morally reprehensible, vulgar, insensitive,
selfish, stupid, you have no taste, a lousy sense of
humour and you smell. You're not even interesting
enough to make me sick.'

Alexandra Medford, *played by* CHER *in* **The Witches Of Eastwick** (1987)

////

'I've got haemorrhoids smarter than you!'

Redeye, *played by* ANDREW DIVOFF *in* **Oblivion** (1994)

'[Married] five times? Wedding bells must sound like an alarm clock to you.'

Tira, *played by* MAE WEST *in* **I'm No Angel** (1933)

∥∥∥

'You have sunk below the deepest layer of prehistoric frog shit at the bottom of a New Jersey scum swamp.'

Oliver Rose, *played by* MICHAEL DOUGLAS *in* **War Of The Roses** (1989)

∥∥∥

'I will put my foot so far up your ass that the water on my knee will quench your thirst.'

Major Benson Payne, *played by* DAMON WAYANS *in* **Major Payne** (1995)

'No one I know of lies with such sincerity.'

John Malcolm, *played by* BURT LANCASTER *in* **Separate Tables** (1958)

IIII

'Sometimes you have to be a high-riding bitch to survive. Sometimes being a bitch is all a woman has to hold on to.'

Vera Donovan, *played by* JUDY PARFITT *in* **Dolores Claiborne** (1995)

'I'm not kind, I'm vicious – it's the secret of my charm.'

Waldo Lydecker, *played by* CLIFTON WEBB *in* **Laura** (1944)

#

'When it gets hot like this, you know what I do? I keep my undies in the icebox!'

The Girl, *played by* MARILYN MONROE *in* **The Seven Year Itch** (1955)

#

'I think you just dislocated my vagina.'

Ruby, *played by* WANDA SYKES *in* **Monster-In-Law** (2005)

'My impotence, my darling, makes a pair with your virginity.'

Miles Brand, *played by* LAURENCE HARVEY *in* **Darling** (1965)

'A dirty mind is a terrible thing to waste.'

Ouiser Boudreaux, *played by* SHIRLEY MACLAINE *in* **Steel Magnolias** (1989)

'You think just because you made a little money you can get a new hairdo and some expensive clothes and turn yourself into a lady. But you can't, because you'll never be anything but a common frump whose father lived over a grocery store and whose mother took in washing.'

Veda Pierce Forrester, *played by* **ANN BLYTH** *in* **Mildred Pierce** (1945)

'I'm not Lassie, I'm not even Dinah Shore. If you want the girl-next-door, go next door!'

Judy Garland, *played by* JUDY DAVIS *in* **Life With Judy Garland: Me And My Shadows** (2001)

////

'God almighty! Someone has sent me a bowel movement.'

Babs Johnson, *played by* DIVINE *in* **Pink Flamingos** (1972)

////

'Lying is the most fun a girl can have without taking her clothes off – but it's better if you do.'

Alice, *played by* NATALIE PORTMAN *in* **Closer** (2004)

'There's something I've always wanted to tell you. You smell like horseshit.'

Alice Baring, *played by* NINA FOCH *in* **Hush** (1998)

'It isn't what you are, it's what you don't become that hurts.'

Sid Jeffers, *played by* OSCAR LEVANT *in* **Humoresque** (1946)

'There's nothing more inconvenient than an old queen with a head cold.'

Toddy Todd, *played by* ROBERT PRESTON *in* **Victor/Victoria** (1982)

'Stealing a man's wife, that's nothing – but stealing a man's car, that's larceny!'

Frank Chambers, *played by* JOHN GARFIELD *in* **The Postman Always Rings Twice** (1946)

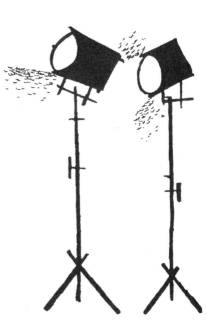

'You wanted advice? Well here it is, straight from me to you. Keep your paws off my underwear.'

Velma Kelly, *played by* CATHERINE ZETA-JONES *in* **Chicago** (2002)

'Now, go and stand somewhere until I need you.'

Cruella De Vil, *played by* **GLENN CLOSE** *in* **101 Dalmatians** (1996)

////

'The details of your incompetence do not interest me.'

Miranda Priestly, *played by* **MERYL STREEP** *in* **The Devil Wears Prada** (2006)

'I always get the fuzzy end of the lollipop.'

Sugar Kane Kowalczyk, *played by* MARILYN MONROE *in* **Some Like It Hot** (1959)

//////

'Think I don't know a due bill when I see one?'

Velma Cruther, *played by* AGNES MOOREHEAD *in* **Hush . . . Hush, Sweet Charlotte** (1964)

//////

'I'm glad you enjoyed it. Now, if you'll excuse me, I have to go unscrew my smile.'

Gracie Hart, *played by* SANDRA BULLOCK *in* **Miss Congeniality** (2000)

'No, we are not friends. I don't take this shit from friends – only lovers.'

Sandy Lester, *played by* TERI GARR *in* **Tootsie** (1982)

////

'I just love finding new places to wear diamonds.'

Lorelei Lee, *played by* MARILYN MONROE *in* **Gentlemen Prefer Blondes** (1953)

////

'Is that what love is? Using people? And maybe that's what hate is – not being able to use people?'

Catherine Holly, *played by* ELIZABETH TAYLOR *in* **Suddenly, Last Summer** (1959)

'Your tongue is old but sharp, Cicero. Be careful how you wag it as one day it will cut off your head.'

Marc Antony, *played by* RICHARD BURTON *in* **Cleopatra** (1963)

⁄ ⁄ ⁄ ⁄

'I'm not living with you! We occupy the same cage, that's all.'

Maggie Pollitt, *played by* ELIZABETH TAYLOR *in* **Cat On A Hot Tin Roof** (1958)

'My understanding of women only goes as far as the pleasure. When it comes to the pain I'm like any other bloke – I don't want to know.'

Alfie Elkins, *played by* **MICHAEL CAINE** *in* **Alfie** (1966)

////

'I accuse you of harlotry! I accuse you of having a scorpion between your legs that seduces men!'

The preacher, *played by* **HARRY NORTHUP** *in* **Bad Girls** (1994)

'No offence, but if that's a woman it looks like she was beaten with an ugly stick.'

Austin Powers, *played by* MIKE MYERS *in* **Austin Powers: International Man Of Mystery** (1997)

# # # #

'Flattery will get you nowhere – but don't stop trying!'

Miss Moneypenny, *played by* LOIS MAXWELL *in* **Dr No** (1962)

# # # #

'There's nothing I love better than a dumb blonde with Daddy's plastic.'

The boutique saleswoman, *played by* LISA KUSHELL *in* **Legally Blonde** (2001)

'What are we, ladies? I'll tell you what we are – waitresses at the banquet of life!'

Mary Rose Foster, *played by* BETTE MIDLER *in* **The Rose** (1979)

''''

'That's quite a dress you almost have on!'

Jerry Mulligan, *played by* GENE KELLY *in* **An American In Paris** (1951)

'The next time you want information, don't scratch for it like a dog – ask for it like a man!'

Steve Dallas, *played by* MARTIN MILNER *in* **Sweet Smell Of Success** (1957)

/ / / /

'You're one to talk, you bloodless, money-grabbing freak!'

Lester Burnham, *played by* KEVIN SPACEY *in* **American Beauty** (1999)

/ / / /

'If I knew I was going to live to 86 I wouldn't have let the maid go.'

Ginny, *played by* KATHARINE HEPBURN *in* **Love Affair** (1994)

'You stick your dick in my mouth and now you get an attack of morality?'

Meredith Johnson, *played by* DEMI MOORE *in* **Disclosure** (1994)

⁄ ⁄ ⁄ ⁄

'I'm tired of men always coming and going, going and coming and always too soon.'

Lily Von Shtupp, *played by* MADELINE KAHN *in* **Blazing Saddles** (1974)

⁄ ⁄ ⁄ ⁄

'Where did she get the shoes? Whores For Less?'

Kelly Lanier Van Ryan, *played by* DENISE RICHARDS *in* **Wild Things** (1998)

'Just what the world needs – another actress.'

Melvin Udall, *played by* JACK NICHOLSON *in* **As Good As It Gets** (1997)

//////

'You have to kiss some ass to get a piece of it.'

Clayton Boone, *played by* BRENDAN FRASER *in* **Gods And Monsters** (1998)

'How great is it for you that I'm not intimidated by your brilliance?'

Dr Julian Mercer, *played by* **KEANU REEVES** *in* **Something's Gotta Give** (2003)

//////

'I hope you bring the cocktail sauce. She's got the crabs, dear, and I don't mean Dungeness.'

Mrs Euphegenia Doubtfire, *played by* **ROBIN WILLIAMS** *in* **Mrs Doubtfire** (1993)

'Don't point that finger at me unless you intend to use it.'

Oscar Madison, *played by* WALTER MATTHAU *in* **The Odd Couple** (1968)

////

'You could park a car in the shadow of his ass!'

Thelma Dickinson, *played by* GEENA DAVIS *in* **Thelma & Louise** (1991)

////

'In my mind, Martha, you're buried in cement, right up to your neck. No, up to your nose, it's much quieter.'

George, *played by* RICHARD BURTON *in* **Who's Afraid Of Virginia Woolf?** (1966)

'If I kept my hair natural like yours, I'd be bald!'

Mame Dennis, *played by* ROSALIND RUSSELL *in* **Auntie Mame** (1958)

////

'I'll admit I may have seen better days, but I'm still not to be had for the price of a cocktail, like a salted peanut.'

Margo Channing, *played by* BETTE DAVIS *in* **All About Eve** (1950)

'I've had hangovers before, but this time even my hair hurts!'

Brad Allen, *played by* ROCK HUDSON *in* **Pillow Talk** (1959)

# # # #

'There's one thing to be said about masturbation – you certainly don't have to look your best.'

Michael, *played by* KENNETH NELSON *in* **The Boys In The Band** (1970)

# # # #

'Is it true when you were born the doctor turned around and slapped your mother?'

Anthony 'Tick' Belrose, *played by* HUGO WEAVING *in* **The Adventures Of Priscilla, Queen Of The Desert** (1994)

'I hated her so much I couldn't get her out of my mind for a minute.'

Johnny Farrell, *played by* GLENN FORD *in* **Gilda** (1946)

/ / / /

'He's not exaggerating a thing, dear, it's all true – every word he isn't saying.'

Johnnie Aysgarth, *played by* CARY GRANT *in* **Suspicion** (1941)

/ / / /

'That's all you've got, lady. Two wrong feet and fucking ugly shoes!'

Erin Brockovich, *played by* JULIA ROBERTS *in* **Erin Brockovich** (2000)

'I simply will not sit down to dinner with Midwestern barbarians, I think too highly of my digestive system.'

Sheridan Whiteside, *played by* MONTY WOOLLEY *in* **The Man Who Came To Dinner** (1942)

'You're looking more like your mother every day. From behind you can really see it.'

Edie Danziger, *played by* SHIRLEY KNIGHT *in* **Diabolique** (1996)

'I wanna be just like you, so I figured all I need is a lobotomy and some tights.'

John Bender, *played by* JUDD NELSON *in* **The Breakfast Club** (1985)

✦✦✦✦

'Women should be kept illiterate and clean, like canaries.'

Phil Whittaker, *played by* ROSCOE KARNS *in* **Woman Of The Year** (1942)

'I do not fear a skunk. I simply do not care for its odour.'

Eula Goodnight, *played by* KATHARINE HEPBURN *in* **Rooster Cogburn**
(1975)

#

'The misery! The exquisite tragedy! The Susan Hayward of it all!'

George Downes, *played by* RUPERT EVERETT *in* **My Best Friend's Wedding**
(1997)

#

'If you're a prince then there's hope for every ape in Africa.'

Geoffrey, *played by* JOHN CASTLE *in* **The Lion In Winter** (1968)

'I would enjoy going out with you . . . if I didn't find you so personally distasteful. You're a sneaky, crude, offensive man. That's just how I feel. I'm sure there are hundreds of girls who admire those qualities.'

Cathy Timberlake, *played by* DORIS DAY *in* **That Touch Of Mink** (1962)

////

'I'm still a star. I never play frumps or virgins.'

Helen Sinclair, *played by* DIANNE WIEST *in* **Bullets Over Broadway** (1994)

////

'Thanks to the silver screen your neurosis has got style.'

Donald, *played by* FREDERICK COMBS *in* **The Boys In The Band** (1970)

'His work is beginning to interfere with his drinking.'

Casey Burke, *played by* OWEN MOORE *in* **A Star Is Born** (1937)

IIII

'It's gorgeous. Let's face it, Roger, that dress is you.'

Max Bialystock, *played by* ZERO MOSTEL *in* **The Producers** (1968)

'I didn't squawk about the steak, dear. I merely said I didn't see that old horse that used to be tethered outside here.'

The Great Man, *played by* WC FIELDS *in* **Never Give A Sucker An Even Break** (1941)

////

'Oh, get back into your kennels, both of you!'

Mitzi Del Bra, *played by* HUGO WEAVING *in* **The Adventures Of Priscilla, Queen Of The Desert** (1994)

////

'You're dead, son. Get yourself buried.'

JJ Hunsecker, *played by* BURT LANCASTER *in* **Sweet Smell Of Success** (1957)

'They say a martini is like a woman's breast – one ain't enough and three is too many.'

Gale, *played by* DORIA COOK *in* **The Parallax View** (1974)

/ / / /

'Whatever Watson has found out, you'll know inevitably. I have unbounded confidence in his lack of discretion.'

Sherlock Holmes, *played by* BASIL RATHBONE *in* **The Adventures Of Sherlock Holmes** (1939)

'I am constantly surprised that women's hats do not provoke more murders.'

Sir Wilfrid Robarts, *played by* CHARLES LAUGHTON *in* **Witness For The Prosecution** (1957)

//////

'It'd be a terrific innovation if you could get your mind to stretch beyond the next wisecrack.'

Terry Randall, *played by* KATHARINE HEPBURN *in* **Stage Door** (1937)

//////

'As long as they've got sidewalks, you've got a job.'

Nan Prescott, *played by* JOAN BLONDELL *in* **Footlight Parade** (1933)

'I wouldn't give you the skin off a grape.'

Tommy Udo, *played by* RICHARD WIDMARK *in* **Kiss Of Death** (1947)

////

'She does more without a voice than anyone I've ever heard!'

Susie Smith, *played by* CELESTE HOLM *in* **Road House** (1948)

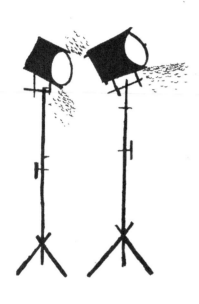

'You look like you've been on a hay ride with Dracula.'

Ruby, *played by* PATRICIA FARR *in* **This Gun For Hire** (1942)

▍▍▍▍

'I hate common sense – it's so common.'

Fiona Gaylord, *played by* BARBARA STANWYCK *in* **The Gay Sisters** (1942)

▍▍▍▍

'Is that your real hair or did you scalp an angel?'

Larry Haines, *played by* BOB HOPE *in* **My Favorite Blonde** (1942)

46

'There is a name for you, ladies, but it isn't used in high society, outside of a kennel.'

Crystal Allen, *played by* JOAN CRAWFORD *in* **The Women** (1939)

/ / / /

'He only lies when he speaks.'

Ella Zielinsky, *played by* GERALDINE CHAPLIN *in* **The Mirror Crack'd** (1980)

/ / / /

'Dying together is even more personal than living together.'

Connie Porter, *played by* TALLULAH BANKHEAD *in* **Lifeboat** (1944)

'I always knew Mother was nothing more than a cheap, hopped-up nymphomaniac.'

Edith Sussman, *played by* NATASHA LYONNE *in* **Die, Mommie, Die!** (2003)

/ / / /

'Politicians are a lot like diapers – they should be changed frequently and for the same reasons.'

Tom Dobbs, *played by* ROBIN WILLIAMS *in* **Man Of The Year** (2006)

/ / / /

'I have been twenty-five for four years, and I shall stay there for another four. Then I'll be twenty-seven for a while. I intend to grow old gracefully.'

Jane Avril, *played by* ZSA ZSA GABOR *in* **Moulin Rouge** (1952)

'In my opinion, most people prefer sardines to caviar because most people haven't tried caviar.'

Rudi Pal, *played by* **ROBERT YOUNG** *in* **The Bride Wore Red** (1937)

⁄⁄⁄⁄

'You're so resourceful, darling, I ought to go to you for plots.'

Nancy Blake, *played by* **FLORENCE NASH** *in* **The Women** (1939)

'Listen, deary, I was at the top when you were a has-been practising to be a never-was!'

Louella Parsons, *played by* ELIZABETH TAYLOR *in* **Malice In Wonderland** (1985)

'Zip that gaping hole of a mouth up, Peggy, before I plug it up with my fist.'

Grizelda Brown, *played by* JEAN HILL *in* **Desperate Living** (1977)

'Throw one at me if you want, hash head. I've got all five senses and I slept last night – that puts me six up on the lot of you.'

Brendan, *played by* JOSEPH GORDON-LEVITT *in* **Brick** (2006)

✼ ✼ ✼

'I distrust a man who says "when". If he's got to be careful not to drink too much, it's because he's not to be trusted when he does.'

Kasper Gutman, *played by* SYDNEY GREENSTREET *in* **The Maltese Falcon** (1941)

✼ ✼ ✼

'Your opinion of me has no cash value.'

Andre Trochard, *played by* BASIL RATHBONE *in* **We're No Angels** (1955)

'Your husband's dead a little over an hour and you're already dressed in black? How long you had that outfit waiting in the closet?'

Lou Peckinpaugh, *played by* PETER FALK *in* **The Cheap Detective** (1978)

////

'If revenge is a dish best served cold, then put on your Sunday finest because it's time to feast!'

Mr. Freeze, *played by* ARNOLD SCHWARZENEGGER *in* **Batman & Robin** (1997)

'You don't have to be alive to be helpful.'

Mathis, *played by* GIANCARLO GIANNINI
in **Casino Royale** (2006)

////

'When I had an ulcer I was farting razor blades.'

Max Goldman, *played by* WALTER MATTHAU
in **Grumpy Old Men** (1993)

////

'Women today are better hung than most men.'

Jonathan Fuerst, *played by* JACK NICHOLSON *in* **Carnal Knowledge** (1971)

'My father used to say that a man can never outdo a woman when it comes to love and revenge.'

Gavin D'Amato, *played by* DANNY DEVITO *in* **War Of The Roses** (1989)

# # # #

'He could use a gift certificate to the Betty Ford Clinic.'

Roland T Flakfizer, *played by* JOHN TURTURRO *in* **Brain Donors** (1992)

# # # #

'We're not fighting! We're in complete agreement! We hate each other!'

Lily Marton, *played by* NANETTE FABRAY *in* **The Band Wagon** (1953)

'Ever since I came here, you've done nothing but treat me like shit. Who the hell do you think you are? Yeah, I was a dance-hall girl, but what makes you so high and mighty? You own a whorehouse! A whorehouse! And with only three whores in it. One of them is just a senile old cow – and the other one's so new at it she doesn't know which end to use.'

Rosie Velez, *played by* DIVINE *in* **Lust In The Dust** (1985]

/ / / /

'A wedding is a funeral where you smell your own flowers!'

Eddie Wilson Jr, *played by* EDDIE CANTOR *in* **Kid Millions** (1934)

'I'll beat you down so far you'll have to roll down your socks to take a shit.'

Sheriff Ed Earl Dodd, *played by* BURT REYNOLDS *in* **The Best Little Whorehouse In Texas** (1982)

////

'I drink because I'm a sensitive and highly strung person.'

Elise Elliot, *played by* GOLDIE HAWN *in* **The First Wives Club** (1996)

////

'I wouldn't have you if you were hung with diamonds upside down!'

Lynn Markham, *played by* JOAN CRAWFORD *in* **Female On The Beach** (1955)

'The last time you were sorry
was when you had to use the pay
toilet and the string on your pet
dime broke.'

Dolores Claiborne, *played by* KATHY BATES *in*
Dolores Claiborne (1995)

////

'Listen, you mealy-mouthed old boot. Are you
totally incapable of saying what you mean?'

June 'George' Buckridge, *played by* BERYL REID *in* **The Killing Of
Sister George** (1968)

'I wouldn't suck your lousy dick if I was suffocating and there was oxygen in your balls!'

Taffy Davenport, *played by* MINK STOLE *in* **Female Trouble** (1974)

IIII

'If you're acting, you're wasting your time. If you're not, you're wasting mine.'

Greg Savitt, *played by* STEVE FORREST *in* **Mommie Dearest** (1981)

'I need you like I need an asshole on my elbow!'

Rupert Guest, *played by* **CLIFTON COLLINS JR** *in* **The Rules Of Attraction** (2002)

//// ////

'A man of few words, all of them long.'

Miles Brand, *played by* **LAURENCE HARVEY** *in* **Darling** (1965)

//// ////

'The important thing is the rhythm. Always have rhythm in your shaking. Now, a Manhattan you shake to foxtrot time, a Bronx to two-step time, a dry martini you always shake to waltz time.'

Nick Charles, *played by* **WILLIAM POWELL** *in* **The Thin Man** (1934)

'My dear girl, you cannot keep bumping your head against reality and saying it is not there.'

Dr Alex Brulov, *played by* MICHAEL CHEKHOV *in* **Spellbound** (1945)

////

'He's a real gentleman! I bet he takes the dishes out of the sink before he pees in it!'

Ouiser Boudreaux, *played by* SHIRLEY MACLAINE *in* **Steel Magnolias** (1989)

////

'How could I have known that murder could sometimes smell like honeysuckle?'

Walter Neff, *played by* FRED MACMURRAY *in* **Double Indemnity** (1944)

'She was a charming middle-aged lady with a face like a bucket of mud. I gave her a drink. She was a gal who'd take a drink – if she had to knock you down to get the bottle.'

Philip Marlowe, *played by* DICK POWELL *in* **Murder, My Sweet** (1944)

# # # #

'Oh yes, I love the smell of near extinction.'

Cruella De Vil, *played by* GLENN CLOSE *in* **101 Dalmatians** (1996)

# # # #

'I would sell my grandmother for a drink – and you know how I love my grandmother.'

Macaulay Connor, *played by* JAMES STEWART *in* **The Philadelphia Story** (1940)

'Come on. Let's get something to eat. I'm thirsty.'

Nick Charles, *played by* WILLIAM POWELL *in* **After The Thin Man** (1936)

# # # #

'Lately you've begun to imagine in
Cinemascope – with stereophonic sound.'

Helen Sherman, *played by* EVELYN KEYES *in* **The Seven Year Itch** (1955)

# # # #

'We women can do things to a man we love that
men wouldn't do to a rattlesnake.'

Fritzi Kiffmeyer, *played by* UNA MERKEL *in* **Saratoga** (1937)

'You wouldn't be a bad-
looking dame if it wasn't
for your face.'

Ruby Adams, *played by* JEAN HARLOW *in*
Hold Your Man (1933)

//////

'You make it a bit too obvious,
you know, that you hate the
very sight of me.'

Ann Shankland, *played by* RITA HAYWORTH
in **Separate Tables** (1958)

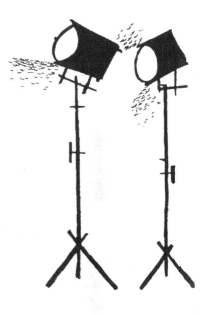

'You're going to end up like a one-legged man in an ass-kicking contest. Useless.'

Cyrus Paice, *played by* MICKEY ROURKE *in* **Get Carter** (2000)

※ ※ ※

'No matter what anyone tells you, it really is the size of your gun that counts.'

Mr Freeze, *played by* ARNOLD SCHWARZENEGGER *in* **Batman & Robin** (1997)

※ ※ ※

'The trick in life isn't getting what you want, my dear, it's wanting it after you get it.'

Ginny, *played by* KATHARINE HEPBURN *in* **Love Affair** (1994)

'My one chance to get raped and you can't even get your bloody trousers off!'

Vicky Allessio, *played by* GLENDA JACKSON *in* **A Touch Of Class** (1973)

////

'Cheap clothes suit you. It's because you're from the gutter.'

Kenneth Halliwell, *played by* ALFRED MOLINA *in* **Prick Up Your Ears** (1987)

'You mustn't get so upset – your facelift is unravelling.'

Louella Parsons, *played by* ELIZABETH TAYLOR *in* **Malice In Wonderland** (1985)

//////

'Alligators have the right idea. They eat their young.'

Ida Corwin, *played by* EVE ARDEN *in* **Mildred Pierce** (1945)

//////

'Which one are you crying about? The predatory prick or the shit-for-brains tramp? Because neither one deserves your tears!'

Amy, *played by* BROOKE SMITH *in* **In Her Shoes** (2005)

'That dame doesn't have a nerve in her body. I don't think her spinal cord touches her brain.'

Julian Marx, *played by* JACK WARDEN *in* **Bullets Over Broadway** (1994)

////

'Poor people are not loved, Arthur, they urinate in public and have very few teeth.'

Hobson, *played by* JOHN GIELGUD *in* **Arthur** (1981)

'To be overly honest in a dishonest world is like plucking a chicken against the wind – you'll only wind up with a mouthful of feathers.'

Moustache, *played by* **LOU JACOBI** *in* **Irma La Douce** (1963)

⁄⁄⁄⁄

'Holy shit! Your hair has a hard-on.'

Mary Rose Foster, *played by* **BETTE MIDLER** *in* **The Rose** (1979)

'We started off on the wrong foot. Let's stay that way!'

Jean Maitland, *played by* GINGER ROGERS *in* **Stage Door** (1937)

////

'Why didn't you just kick him in the balls and tell him he has ugly children?'

Marty, *played by* PETER MACNICOL *in* **HouseSitter** (1992)

////

'Shouldn't you be holding the crucifix? It is *the* prop for martyrs!'

Armand Goldman, *played by* ROBIN WILLIAMS *in* **The Birdcage** (1996)

'Louie brought his new girlfriend over and the nicest thing I can say about her is all her tattoos are spelled correctly.'

Truvy Jones, *played by* **DOLLY PARTON** *in* **Steel Magnolias** (1989)

/ / / /

'Well this whole world stinks, Francine, so get used to it. You and that big nose of yours are startin' to get on my nerves. Snortin' around the place like a goddamned anteater. I've just about had it with you. Gimme that drink! Hurry up!'

Elmer Fishpaw, *played by* **DAVID SAMSON** *in* **Polyester** (1981)

'Sometimes the shit comes down so heavy I feel
I should be wearing a hard hat.'

Ned Racine, *played by* WILLIAM HURT *in* **Body Heat** (1981)

///

'You're all I thought about for six months. They
threw me in a jail filled with rejects from the
communicable disease ward. Every wacko, drippy,
open-sored low-life was in that joint, all of them
wanting to hire on as my proctologist.'

Ralph, *played by* DANNY DEVITO *in* **The Jewel Of The Nile** (1985)

///

'Don't touch me unless you love me.'

Joseph Frady, *played by* WARREN BEATTY *in* **The Parallax View** (1974)

'He has an empty stomach and it's gone to his head!'

Joe, *played by* **TONY CURTIS** *in* **Some Like It Hot** (1959)

*/ */ */ */

'Before I started doing drugs, I had so many
problems. Now I only have one. Drugs. I have
a focus now.'

Lyle, *played by* **ADRIAN GRENIER** *in* **Cecil B Demented** (2000)

*/ */ */ */

'What did you do, wake up this morning and say,
"Today I'm going to ruin a man's life?"'

Jack T Colton, *played by* **MICHAEL DOUGLAS** *in* **Romancing The Stone**
(1984)

'Oh my God, what a horrible photograph. My first wanted poster and I look just awful.'

Babs Johnson, *played by* DIVINE *in* **Pink Flamingos** (1972)

    IIII

'I just remembered – I have an appointment with a headache.'

Martha Gray, *played by* MARSHA HUNT *in* **Smash-Up** (1947)

'You've got the complexion of a gravel pit.'

Leopold Dilg, *played by* CARY GRANT *in* **The Talk Of The Town** (1942)

////

'How can one man be so endlessly disappointing?'

Alice, *played by* NATALIE PORTMAN *in* **Closer** (2004)

////

'You stupid woman, I didn't have you sacked. If you'd have taken the time to read the confidential material you stole from my briefcase, you know that you were dismissed because you're a fat boring actress and people are sick to death of you.'

Mercy Croft, *played by* CORAL BROWNE *in* **The Killing Of Sister George** (1968)

'You're dumber than you think I think you are.'

Jake Gittes, *played by* JACK NICHOLSON *in* **Chinatown** (1974)

/ / / /

'The cheaper the crook, the
gaudier the patter.'

Sam Spade, *played by* HUMPHREY BOGART
in **The Maltese Falcon** (1941)

/ / / /

'Death by mini-bar, how
glamorous!'

George Downes, *played by* RUPERT EVERETT
in **My Best Friend's Wedding** (1997)

'You're still a shit sandwich. You're just not a soggy one. From this moment, you are no longer turds. You have graduated to maggots!'

Major Benson Payne, *played by* DAMON WAYANS *in* **Major Payne** (1995)

////

'She could use some mascara and some serious highlights, but she's not completely unfortunate looking.'

Elle Woods, *played by* REESE WITHERSPOON *in* **Legally Blonde** (2001)

'Well, cut off my legs and call me Shorty.'

Brogan, *played by* EDWARD BROPHY *in* **The Thin Man Goes Home** (1944)

# # # #

'Fix your hair – you look like a damn cockatoo.'

Ruby, *played by* WANDA SYKES *in* **Monster-In-Law** (2005)

# # # #

'You know, Norman, you really are the sweetest man in the world, but I'm the only one that knows it.'

Ethel Thayer, *played by* KATHARINE HEPBURN *in* **On Golden Pond** (1981)

'Most women use more brains picking a horse in the third at Belmont than they do picking a husband.'

Schatze Page, *played by* LAUREN BACALL *in* **How To Marry A Millionaire** (1953)

////

'What's the decor? Early Mexican brothel?'

Armande Voizin, *played by* JUDI DENCH *in* **Chocolat** (2000)

////

'You do make a better impression with your clothes off.'

Jackson Baring, *played by* JONATHAN SCHAECH *in* **Hush** (1998)

'I envy people who drink. At least they know what to blame everything on.'

Sid Jeffers, *played by* OSCAR LEVANT *in* **Humoresque** (1946)

# # # #

'I know him – he's too nervous to kill himself. Why, he even wears a seatbelt at drive-in movies.'

Oscar Madison, *played by* WALTER MATTHAU *in* **The Odd Couple** (1968)

'Tell me, Mrs Wright, does your husband interfere with your marriage?'

Sid Jeffers, *played by* OSCAR LEVANT *in* **Humoresque** (1946)

////

'Grow up, Heather, bulimia is so '87.'

Heather Chandler, *played by* KIM WALKER *in* **Heathers** (1989)

'You and your rabbit-faced wife can go to hell.'

Amanda Farrow, *played by* JOAN CRAWFORD *in* **The Best Of Everything**
(1959)

//////

'Is this how we dress for the office? You look like
a blood clot!'

Sadie Shelton, *played by* BETTE MIDLER *in* **Big Business** (1988)

//////

'Lawyers should never marry other lawyers. This is
called inbreeding, from which comes idiot children
and other lawyers.'

Kip Lurie, *played by* DAVID WAYNE *in* **Adam's Rib** (1949)

'Get up! You think you're an alley cat dropping its litter by the side of the road?'

Martha Baring, *played by* JESSICA LANGE *in* **Hush** (1998)

░ ░ ░ ░

'My dear, either you were born in an extremely rustic community where good manners are unknown, or you suffer from a common feminine delusion that the mere fact of being a woman exempts you from the rules of civilised conduct.'

Waldo Lydecker, *played by* CLIFTON WEBB *in* **Laura** (1944)

'But enough about me, let's talk about you – what do you think about me?'

CC Bloom, *played by* BETTE MIDLER *in* **Beaches** (1988)

/ / / /

'With my brains and your looks, we could go places.'

Frank Chambers, *played by* JOHN GARFIELD *in* **The Postman Always Rings Twice** (1946)

/ / / /

'Who needs him? I've got a vibrator.'

Mary Jensen, *played by* CAMERON DIAZ *in* **There's Something About Mary** (1998)

'She's like Satan in heels!'

Fern Mayo, *played by* JUDY GREER *in* **Jawbreaker** (1999)

////

'I'd hate to take a bite outta you. You're a cookie full of arsenic.'

JJ Hunsecker, *played by* BURT LANCASTER *in* **Sweet Smell Of Success** (1957)

////

'Good luck doesn't happen to people like us. Good luck happens to Madonna.'

Rona Mace, *played by* JAMIE LEE CURTIS *in* **Drowning Mona** (2000)

'Why, I'm so mean I even hate myself.'

Peter Potter Jr, *played by* **BOB HOPE** *in* **Son Of Paleface** (1952)

/ / / /

'Do you have any control over how creepy you allow yourself to get?'

Carol Connolly, *played by* **HELEN HUNT** *in* **As Good As It Gets** (1997)

'Everything you touch turns to rigor mortis.'

Ronnie Jackson, *played by* **BOB HOPE** *in* **My Favorite Brunette** (1947)

/ / / /

'I have the feeling this is going to be the beginning of a beautiful hatred.'

Geoffrey Carroll, *played by* **HUMPHREY BOGART** *in* **The Two Mrs Carrolls** (1947)

/ / / /

'I can be smart when I need to be.'

Lorelei Lee, *played by* **MARILYN MONROE** *in* **Gentlemen Prefer Blondes** (1953)

'So you got pinched in the elevator. So what? Would you rather be picking lead out of your navel?'

Joe, *played by* TONY CURTIS *in* **Some Like It Hot** (1959)

////

'Dreams? I'm having nightmares in Cinemascope!'

Connie Jones, *played by* JEANNE CRAIN *in* **Gentlemen Marry Brunettes** (1955)

////

'You're so mean, if it were raining hundred-dollar bills, you'd be out looking for a dime you lost someplace.'

Ann Mitchell, *played by* BARBARA STANWYCK *in* **Meet John Doe** (1941)

'Can I interest you in a turn-on?'

Lance Lawson, *played by* ERIC STOLTZ *in* **The Rules Of Attraction** (2002)

////

'A woman happily in love, she burns the soufflé. A woman unhappily in love, she forgets to turn on the oven.'

Baron St Fontanel, *played by* MARCEL DALIO *in* **Sabrina** (1954)

'Well cheer up, Mary, living alone has its compensations. Heaven knows, it's marvellous being able to spread out in bed like a swastika.'

Mrs Moorehead, *played by* LUCILE WATSON *in* **The Women** (1939)

✳ ✳ ✳

'How extravagant you are, throwing away women like that. Some day they may be scarce.'

Captain Renault, *played by* CLAUDE RAINS *in* **Casablanca** (1942)

✳ ✳ ✳

'I'm gonna kick your ass so hard you'll have to unbutton your collar to shit.'

Inspector Harry Callahan, *played by* CLINT EASTWOOD *in* **The Dead Pool** (1988)

'Oh, why don't you grow feathers and go shit in a tree?'

Gwen Phillips, *played by* **GOLDIE HAWN** *in* **HouseSitter** (1992)

////

'If you wanted a babysitter you should've married Mary Poppins.'

Suzanne Stone Maretto, *played by* **NICOLE KIDMAN** *in* **To Die For** (1995)

////

'Oh, Sammy's so confused, he don't know whether to scratch his watch or wind his butt.'

Truvy Jones, *played by* **DOLLY PARTON** *in* **Steel Magnolias** (1989)

'Thanks for the compliment, but I know how I look. This is the way I look when I'm sober. It's enough to make a person drink, wouldn't you say?'

Kirsten Arnesen Clay, *played by* LEE REMICK *in* **Days Of Wine And Roses** (1962)

////

'I'm going to attach a pine cone to my vibrator and have a really merry Christmas.'

Bobbie Markowitz, *played by* BETTE MIDLER *in* **The Stepford Wives** (2004)

'At first I thought he was walking his dog. Then I realised – it was his date.'

Cuddles Kovinsky, *played by* **EDITH MASSEY** *in* **Polyester** (1981)

////

'You obviously have a wonderful economy with words, Gloria – I look forward to your next syllable with great eagerness.'

Hobson, *played by* **JOHN GIELGUD** *in* **Arthur** (1981)

'Curls weren't a good look for her . . . she didn't have the bone structure.'

Elle Woods, *played by* REESE WITHERSPOON *in* **Legally Blonde** (2001)

//// //

'You simply must see my hairdresser – I detest whoever does yours.'

Sylvia, *played by* ROSALIND RUSSELL *in* **The Women** (1939)

//// //

'I'm so glad to see that you've not only kept your gorgeous figure, but you've added so much to it!'

Lola Brewster, *played by* KIM NOVAK *in* **The Mirror Crack'd** (1980)

'I know exactly how you feel, my dear. The morning after always looks grim if you happen to be wearing last night's dress.'

Grand Duchess Swana, *played by* INA CLAIRE *in* **Ninotchka** (1939)

/ / / /

'I marvel at you after all these years. Still like a democratic drawbridge – going down for everybody.'

Henry II, *played by* PETER O'TOOLE *in* **The Lion In Winter** (1968)

'I swear, that queen gives me
gas.'

Bertha Venation, *played by* CHARLES PIERCE
in **Torch Song Trilogy** (1988)

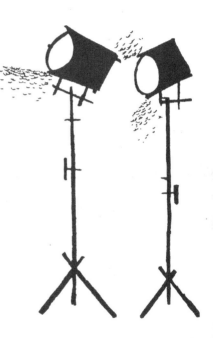

'Oh, it reeks of taste.'

Mrs Euphegenia Doubtfire, *played by*
ROBIN WILLIAMS *in* **Mrs Doubtfire** (1993)

'I can never get a zipper to
close. Maybe that stands for
something.'

Gilda Mundson Farrell, *played by* RITA HAYWORTH *in* **Gilda** (1946)

'I'm telling you, if I didn't have a dress on, I'd kick his arrogant ass in.'

Dorothy Michaels, *played by* DUSTIN HOFFMAN *in* **Tootsie** (1982)

//////

'He's so low that when they bury him, they'll have to dig up!'

Connie Emerson, *played by* AUDREY MEADOWS *in* **That Touch Of Mink** (1962)

//////

'It's been a quarter of a century since you've gone to bed with anything other than a hot-water bottle.'

Louella Parsons, *played by* ELIZABETH TAYLOR *in* **Malice In Wonderland** (1985)

'Congratulations – you've just won gold, silver and bronze in the moron Olympics!'

Cruella De Vil, *played by* GLENN CLOSE *in* **101 Dalmatians** (1996)

////

'That's a B. It's the first letter of a seven-letter word that means your father.'

Mame Dennis, *played by* ROSALIND RUSSELL *in* **Auntie Mame** (1958)

'Don't stomp your little last-season Prada shoes at me, honey!'

Enrique Salvatore, *played by* GREG SERANO *in* **Legally Blonde** (2001)

////

'Let's get one thing straight first: a) I want a child, and b) if anyone asks, I'm the pretty one.'

Arnold, *played by* HARVEY FIERSTEIN *in* **Torch Song Trilogy** (1988)

'Don't make it sound like such a threat. Being thrown out of a place like this is significantly better than being thrown out of a leper colony.'

Toddy Todd, *played by* ROBERT PRESTON *in* **Victor/Victoria** (1982)

//// ////

'For a butcher's daughter you sure don't mince words.'

Louella Parsons, *played by* ELIZABETH TAYLOR *in* **Malice In Wonderland** (1985)

//// ////

'I'm supposed to be the grand duchess Anastasia, but I think I look more like Tugboat Annie.'

Roger De Bris, *played by* CHRISTOPHER HEWETT *in* **The Producers** (1968)

'Bore someone else with your questions.'

Miranda Priestly, *played by* MERYL STREEP *in* **The Devil Wears Prada** (2006)

/ / / /

'Getting dolled up is easy – it's looking natural that takes time.'

Kate Palmer, *played by* LEE REMICK *in* **No Way To Treat A Lady** (1968)

/ / / /

'Now you know why drag queens drink from such big glasses! To make their hands look smaller!'

Marion, *played by* SARAH CHADWICK *in* **The Adventures Of Priscilla, Queen Of The Desert** (1994)

'I think the greatest harm done to the human race has been done by the poets. They keep filling people's heads with delusions about love, writing about it as if it were a symphony orchestra or a flight of angels.'

Dr Constance Petersen, *played by* **INGRID BERGMAN** *in* **Spellbound** (1945)

/ / / /

'Oh, I have napkins that match your hat.'

Sunny Davis, *played by* **GOLDIE HAWN** *in* **Protocol** (1984)

"'Okay, Marlowe," I said to myself, "you're a tough guy. You've been sapped twice, choked, beaten silly with a gun, shot in the arm until you're crazy as a couple of waltzing mice. Now let's see you do something really tough – like putting your pants on.'"

Philip Marlowe, *played by* **DICK POWELL** *in* **Murder, My Sweet** (1944)

/ / / /

'When you're in love with a married man, you should never wear mascara.'

Fran Kubelik, *played by* **SHIRLEY MACLAINE** *in* **The Apartment** (1960)

'Nice hairdo. You get FM on that?'

Winston Connelly, *played by* KEANU REEVES *in* **The Night Before** (1988)

/ / / /

'If that dress had pockets, you'd look like a pool table.'

Thornton Melon, *played by* RODNEY DANGERFIELD *in* **Back To School** (1986)

/ / / /

'Oh you poor, poor dear. You could have married Elliot Firestone, the man who invented the wheel. Instead you married Fred Flintstone, the man who invented the excuse.'

Pearl Slaghoople, *played by* ELIZABETH TAYLOR *in* **The Flintstones** (1994)

'I can't believe this – both my boyfriends are cheating on me!'

Suzanna, *played by* HEATHER GRAHAM *in* **Don't Do It!** (1994)

I I I I

'Your idea of fidelity is not having more than one man in bed at the same time.'

Robert Gold, *played by* DIRK BOGARDE *in* **Darling** (1965)

'When you've got a hump back, why spend money on a nose job?'

Pearl Berman, *played by* SHIRLEY MACLAINE *in* **Used People** (1992)

/ / / /

'I like my sex the way I play basketball – one-on-one with as little dribbling as possible.'

Lieutenant Frank Drebin, *played by* LESLIE NIELSEN *in* **Naked Gun 33⅓: The Final Insult** (1993)

/ / / /

'I see that, in addition to your other charms, you have that insolence generated by an unfair upbringing.'

Terry Randall, *played by* KATHARINE HEPBURN *in* **Stage Door** (1937)

'Could you sweat the other way, please?'

Walter Fielding Jr, *played by* TOM HANKS *in* **The Money Pit** (1986)

§ § § §

'She's the village bicycle – everyone's had a ride.'

Austin Powers, *played by* MIKE MYERS *in* **Austin Powers: International Man Of Mystery** (1997)

§ § § §

'I need you to take your ego out of the equation.'

M, *played by* JUDI DENCH *in* **Casino Royale** (2006)

'I barely have time to keep a journal, let alone breastfeed an orphan!'

Katya Livingston, *played by* JENNIFER LOVE HEWITT *in* **Confessions Of A Sociopathic Social Climber** (2005)

////

'Way down deep he's very superficial.'

Dorothy Parker, *played by* ROSEMARY MURPHY *in* **Julia** (1977)

////

'You're so deceitful . . . we could tangle spiders in the webs you weave.'

Richard, *played by* ANTHONY HOPKINS *in* **The Lion In Winter** (1968)

'Life is short but marriage is long – so drink up, it'll make it go a hell of a lot faster.'

Katharine Richelieu, *played by* SHIRLEY MACLAINE *in* **Rumour Has It** (2005)

///

'Haven't you got any more sense than to shout at me like that?'

Clyde Wynant, *played by* EDWARD ELLIS *in* **The Thin Man** (1934)

///

'Opinions are like assholes – everybody's got one.'

Inspector Harry Callahan, *played by* CLINT EASTWOOD *in* **The Dead Pool** (1988)

'I bet she drinks from the bottle.'

Barton Keyes, *played by* EDWARD G ROBINSON *in* **Double Indemnity** (1944)

//////

'I've got myself a pretty good bullshit detector, and I can tell when somebody's peeing on my boots and telling me it's a rainstorm.'

Sheriff Ed Earl Dodd, *played by* BURT REYNOLDS *in* **The Best Little Whorehouse In Texas** (1982)

'When it comes to pain and suffering, she's right up there with Elizabeth Taylor!'

Truvy Jones, *played by* DOLLY PARTON *in* **Steel Magnolias** (1989)

////

'The cat's in the bag and the bag's in the river.'

Sidney Falco, *played by* TONY CURTIS *in* **Sweet Smell Of Success** (1957)

'When I get back to my room the only thing I want to find missing is you!'

Jean Maitland, *played by* GINGER ROGERS *in* **Stage Door** (1937)

////

'Do you notice I'm limping? Spilled a hot drink down my dress. My vagina came up like a football.'

Mrs Sugden, *played by* JANET DALE *in* **Prick Up Your Ears** (1987)

////

'First of all, I should like to say that I think the arguments advanced by the counsel for the defence were sound – mere sound!'

Adam Bonner, *played by* SPENCER TRACY *in* **Adam's Rib** (1949)

'Don't be ridiculous! Jack would never die without telling me first.'

Joan Wilder, *played by* KATHLEEN TURNER *in* **The Jewel Of The Nile** (1985)

/ / / /

'Tell me, which lunatic asylum did they get you out of?'

James Bond, *played by* SEAN CONNERY *in* **From Russia With Love** (1963)

/ / / /

'I didn't kill that bitch any more than I'm wearing a diamond tiara.'

Dolores Claiborne, *played by* KATHY BATES *in* **Dolores Claiborne** (1995)

'I don't go to church. Kneeling bags my nylons.'

Lorraine Mimosa, *played by* JAN STERLING *in* **Ace In The Hole** (1951)

////

'My dad thinks I paid for all this with catering jobs.
Never underestimate the power of denial.'

Ricky Fitts, *played by* WES BENTLEY *in* **American Beauty** (1999)

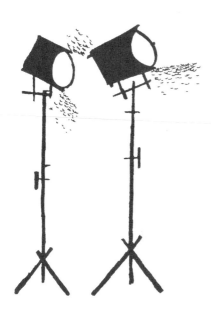

'Vulgarity has its uses.'

Mrs Jescott, *played by* **CARMEN MATHEWS** *in* **Butterfield 8** (1960)

'"You look tired" means you look old. "You look rested" means you've had collagen.'

Albert Goldman, *played by* **NATHAN LANE** *in* **The Birdcage** (1996)

'When I look at you I know what I want to avoid.'

Paul Boray, *played by* JOHN GARFIELD *in* **Humoresque** (1946)

/ / / /

'Poor Winston's idea of foreplay was, "Brace
yourself, Effie."'

Mrs Euphegenia Doubtfire, *played by* ROBIN WILLIAMS *in* **Mrs Doubtfire**
(1993)

/ / / /

'Why don't you just light your tampon and blow
your box apart? Because it's the only bang you're
ever gonna get, sweetheart!'

Bernadette Bassenger, *played by* TERENCE STAMP *in* **The Adventures Of
Priscilla, Queen Of the Desert** (1994)

'It's one thing to want someone out of your life, but it's another thing to serve them a wake-up cup full of liquid drainer.'

Veronica Sawyer, *played by* WINONA RYDER *in* **Heathers** (1989)

❊ ❊ ❊

'The last time I had a pap smear, the guy needed leather gloves and an oyster shucker.'

Magda, *played by* LIN SHAYE *in* **There's Something About Mary** (1998)

❊ ❊ ❊

'If my dog was as ugly as you, I'd shave his ass and teach him to walk backwards.'

Max Goldman, *played by* WALTER MATTHAU *in* **Grumpier Old Men** (1995)

'You forgot your fortune cookie.
It says "You're shit outta luck."'

Inspector Harry Callahan, *played by* **CLINT
EASTWOOD** *in* **The Dead Pool** (1988)

∥ ∥ ∥

'What a nasty streak you have
when you drink. Also when you
eat and sit and walk.'

Sidney Cochran, *played by* **MICHAEL CAINE**
in **California Suite** (1978)

'You're looking great. Who's your embalmer?'

Diane Moody, *played by* JULIETTE LEWIS *in* **The Basketball Diaries** (1995)

////

'I was in love with a beautiful blonde once, dear. She drove me to drink. That's the one thing I'm indebted to her for.'

The Great Man, *played by* WC FIELDS *in* **Never Give A Sucker An Even Break** (1941)

'If I give you any more collagen your lips are going to look like they got stuck in a pool drain.'

Dr Morris Packman, *played by* ROB REINER *in* **The First Wives Club** (1996)

❙ ❙ ❙ ❙

'You're the Ernest Hemingway of bullshit!'

Newton Davis, *played by* STEVE MARTIN *in* **HouseSitter** (1992)

❙ ❙ ❙ ❙

'I ain't still mad . . . this here is brand new mad!'

Arnold, *played by* HARVEY FIERSTEIN *in* **Torch Song Trilogy** (1988)

'Get your fishhooks off me!'

Sheridan Whiteside, *played by* MONTY WOOLLEY *in* **The Man Who Came To Dinner** (1942)

////

'The last time I saw a walk like that was in *Jurassic Park*.'

Victor Melling, *played by* MICHAEL CAINE *in* **Miss Congeniality** (2000)

'Chin up, darling. Both of them!'

Lola Brewster, *played by* KIM NOVAK *in* **The Mirror Crack'd** (1980)

/ / / /

'From the back she looks like a fridge with a head.'

Kenny Smyth, *played by* SHANE JACOBSON *in* **Kenny** (2006)

/ / / /

'Did you have a brain tumour for breakfast?'

Heather Chandler, *played by* KIM WALKER *in* **Heathers** (1989)

'Doesn't that bird brain of yours ever function?'

Sheridan Whiteside, *played by* MONTY WOOLLEY *in* **The Man Who Came To Dinner** (1942)

# # # #

'Don't let him frighten you. He has a heart of gold – only harder!'

Oliver Niles, *played by* ADOLPHE MENJOU *in* **A Star Is Born** (1937)

# # # #

'Does Barry Manilow know you raided his wardrobe?'

John Bender, *played by* JUDD NELSON *in* **The Breakfast Club** (1985)

'You're like some fancy kind of disease. I had it once but now I'm immune.'

Judson Prentiss, *played by* JOHN IRELAND *in* **Queen Bee** (1955)

/ / / /

'In that wig, you could play Lassie.'

Marina Rudd, *played by* ELIZABETH TAYLOR *in* **The Mirror Crack'd** (1980)

/ / / /

'Explain it to the fattier end of my baseball bat.'

Hattie Mae Pierce, *played by* ELLA MITCHELL *in* **Big Momma's House** (2000)

'What's the difference between a light bulb and a pregnant woman? You can unscrew a light bulb.'

Vinnie Antonelli, *played by* STEVE MARTIN *in* **My Blue Heaven** (1990)

'You're not dead yet, so stop living as if you are!'

CC Bloom, *played by* BETTE MIDLER *in* **Beaches** (1988)

MOVIES CITED

Ace In The Hole
Directed by Billy Wilder, 1951

Adam's Rib
Directed by George Cukor, 1949

The Adventures Of Priscilla, Queen Of The Desert
Directed by Stephan Elliott, 1994

The Adventures Of Sherlock Holmes
Directed by Alfred L Werker, 1939

After The Thin Man
Directed by WS Van Dyke, 1936

Alfie
Directed by Lewis Gilbert, 1966

All About Eve
Directed by Joseph L Mankiewicz, 1950

American Beauty
Directed by Sam Mendes, 1999

An American In Paris
Directed by Vincente Minnelli, 1951

The Apartment
Directed by Billy Wilder, 1960

The Arrangement
Directed by Elia Kazan, 1969

Arthur
Directed by Steve Gordon, 1981

As Good As It Gets
Directed by James L Brooks, 1997

Auntie Mame
Directed by Morton DaCosta, 1958

Austin Powers: International Man Of Mystery
Directed by Jay Roach, 1997

Autumn Leaves
Directed by Robert Aldrich, 1956

Back To School
Directed by Alan Metter, 1986

Bad Girls
Directed by Jonathan Kaplan, 1994

The Band Wagon
Directed by Vincente Minnelli, 1953

The Basketball Diaries
Directed by Scott Kalvert, 1995

Batman & Robin
Directed by Joel Schumacher, 1997

Beaches
Directed by Garry Marshall, 1988

The Best Little Whorehouse In Texas
Directed by Colin Higgins, 1982

The Best Of Everything
Directed by Jean Negulesco, 1959

Big Business
Directed by Jim Abrahams, 1988

Big Momma's House
Directed by Raja Gosnell, 2000

The Birdcage
Directed by Mike Nichols, 1996

Blazing Saddles
Directed by Mel Brooks, 1974

Body Heat
Directed by Lawrence Kasdan, 1981

The Boys In The Band
Directed by William Friedkin, 1970

Brain Donors
Directed by Dennis Dugan, 1992

The Breakfast Club
Directed by John Hughes, 1985

Brick
Directed by Rian Johnson, 2006

The Bride Wore Red
Directed by Dorothy Arzner, 1937

Bullets Over Broadway
Directed by Woody Allen, 1994

Butterfield 8
Directed by Daniel Mann, 1960

The Cabin In The Cotton
Directed by Michael Curtiz, 1932

California Suite
Directed by Herbert Ross, 1978

Carnal Knowledge
Directed by Mike Nichols, 1971

Casablanca
Directed by Michael Curtiz, 1942

Casino Royale
Directed by Martin Campbell, 2006

Cat On A Hot Tin Roof
Directed by Richard Brooks, 1958

Cecil B Demented
Directed by John Waters, 2000

The Cheap Detective
Directed by Robert Moore, 1978

Chicago
Directed by Rob Marshall, 2002

Chinatown
Directed by Roman Polanski, 1974

Chocolat
Directed by Lasse Hallström, 2000

Cleopatra
Directed by Joseph L Mankiewicz, 1963

Closer
Directed by Mike Nichols, 2004

Confessions Of A Sociopathic Social Climber
Directed by Dana Lustig, 2005

Darling
Directed by John Schlesinger, 1965

Days Of Wine And Roses
Directed by Blake Edwards, 1962

The Dead Pool
Directed by Buddy Van Horn, 1988

Desperate Living
Directed by John Waters, 1977

The Devil Wears Prada
Directed by David Frankel, 2006

Diabolique
Directed by Jeremiah Chechik, 1996

Die, Mommie, Die!
Directed by Mark Rucker, 2003

Dinner At Eight
Directed by George Cukor, 1933

Disclosure
Directed by Barry Levinson, 1994

Dolores Claiborne
Directed by Taylor Hackford, 1995

Don't Do It!
Directed by Eugene Hess, 1994

Double Indemnity
Directed by Billy Wilder, 1944

Dr No
Directed by Terence Young, 1962

Drowning Mona
Directed by Nick Gomez, 2000

Erin Brockovich
Directed by Steven Soderbergh, 2000

Female On The Beach
Directed by Joseph Pevney, 1955

Female Trouble
Directed by John Waters, 1974

The First Wives Club
Directed by Hugh Wilson, 1996

The Flintstones
Directed by Brian Levant, 1994

Footlight Parade
Directed by Lloyd Bacon, 1933

From Russia With Love
Directed by Terence Young, 1963

The Gay Sisters
Directed by Irving Rapper, 1942

Gentlemen Marry Brunettes
Directed by Richard Sale, 1955

Gentlemen Prefer Blondes
Directed by Howard Hawkes, 1953

Get Carter
Directed by Stephen Kay, 2000

Gilda
Directed by Charles Vidor, 1946

Gods And Monsters
Directed by Bill Condon, 1998

Gone With The Wind
Directed by Victor Fleming, 1939

Grumpier Old Men
Directed by Howard Deutch, 1995

Grumpy Old Men
Directed by Donald Petrie, 1993

Heathers
Directed by Michael Lehmann, 1989

Hold Your Man
Directed by Sam Wood, 1933

HouseSitter
Directed by Frank Oz, 1992

How To Marry A Millionaire
Directed by Jean Negulesco, 1953

Humoresque
Directed by Jean Negulesco, 1946

Hush
Directed by Jonathan Darby, 1998

Hush . . . Hush, Sweet Charlotte
Directed by Robert Aldrich, 1964

I'm No Angel
Directed by Wesley Ruggles, 1933

In Her Shoes
Directed by Curtis Hanson, 2005

Irma La Douce
Directed by Billy Wilder, 1963

Jawbreaker
Directed by Darren Stein, 1999

The Jewel Of The Nile
Directed by Lewis Teague, 1985

Julia
Directed by Fred Zinnemann, 1977

Kenny
Directed by Clayton Jacobson, 2006

Kid Millions
Directed by Roy Del Ruth, 1934

The Killing Of Sister George
Directed by Robert Aldrich, 1968

Kiss Of Death
Directed by Henry Hathaway, 1947

Lantana
Directed by Ray Lawrence, 2001

Laura
Directed by Otto Preminger, 1944

Legally Blonde
Directed by Robert Luketic, 2001

Life With Judy Garland: Me And My Shadows
Directed by Robert Allan Ackerman, 2001

Lifeboat
Directed by Alfred Hitchcock, 1944

The Lion In Winter
Directed by Anthony Harvey, 1968

Love Affair
Directed by Glenn Gordon Caron, 1994

Lust In The Dust
Directed by Paul Bartel, 1985

Major Payne
Directed by Nick Castle, 1995

Malice In Wonderland
Directed by Gus Trikonis, 1985

The Maltese Falcon
Directed by John Huston, 1941

Man Of The Year
Directed by Barry Levinson, 2006

The Man Who Came To Dinner
Directed by William Keighley, 1942

Meet John Doe
Directed by Frank Capra, 1941

Mildred Pierce
Directed by Michael Curtiz, 1945

The Mirror Crack'd
Directed by Guy Hamilton, 1980

Miss Congeniality
Directed by Donald Petrie, 2000

Mommie Dearest
Directed by Frank Perry, 1981

The Money Pit
Directed by Richard Benjamin, 1986

Monster-In-Law
Directed by Robert Luketic, 2005

Moulin Rouge
Directed by John Huston, 1952

Mrs Doubtfire
Directed by Chris Columbus, 1993

Murder, My Sweet
Directed by Edward Dmytryk, 1944

Muriel's Wedding
Directed by PJ Hogan, 1994

My Beautiful Laundrette
Directed by Stephen Frears, 1985

My Best Friend's Wedding
Directed by PJ Hogan, 1997

My Blue Heaven
Directed by Herbert Ross, 1990

My Favorite Blonde
Directed by Sidney Lanfield, 1942

My Favorite Brunette
Directed by Elliott Nugent, 1947

Naked Gun 33 ⅓: The Final Insult
Directed by Peter Segal, 1993

Never Give A Sucker An Even Break
Directed by Edward F Cline, 1941

The Night Before
Directed by Thom Eberhardt, 1988

Ninotchka
Directed by Ernst Lubitsch, 1939

No Way To Treat A Lady
Directed by Jack Smight, 1968

Oblivion
Directed by Sam Irvin, 1994

The Odd Couple
Directed by Gene Saks, 1968

101 Dalmatians
Directed by Stephen Herek, 1996

On Golden Pond
Directed by Mark Rydell, 1981

The Parallax View
Directed by Alan J Pakula, 1974

The Perils Of Pauline
Directed by George Marshall, 1947

The Philadelphia Story
Directed by George Cukor, 1940

Pillow Talk
Directed by Michael Gordon, 1959

Pink Flamingos
Directed by John Waters, 1972

Polyester
Directed by John Waters, 1981

The Postman Always Rings Twice
Directed by Tay Garnett, 1946

Prick Up Your Ears
Directed by Stephen Frears, 1987

The Producers
Directed by Mel Brooks, 1968

Protocol
Directed by Herbert Ross, 1984

Queen Bee
Directed by Ranald MacDougall, 1955

Road House
Directed by Jean Negulesco, 1948

Romancing The Stone
Directed by Robert Zemeckis, 1984

Rooster Cogburn
Directed by Stuart Millar, 1975

The Rose
Directed by Mark Rydell, 1979

The Rules Of Attraction
Directed by Roger Avary, 2002

Rumour Has It
Directed by Rob Reiner, 2005

Sabrina
Directed by Billy Wilder, 1954

Saratoga
Directed by Jack Conway, 1937

Separate Tables
Directed by Delbert Mann, 1958

The Seven Year Itch
Directed by Billy Wilder, 1955

Smash-Up
Directed by Stuart Heisler, 1947

Some Like It Hot
Directed by Billy Wilder, 1959

Something's Gotta Give
Directed by Nancy Meyers, 2003

Son Of Paleface
Directed by Frank Tashlin, 1952

Spellbound
Directed by Alfred Hitchcock, 1945

Stage Door
Directed by Gregory La Cava, 1937

A Star Is Born
Directed by William A Wellman, 1937

Steel Magnolias
Directed by Herbert Ross, 1989

The Stepford Wives
Directed by Frank Oz, 2004

Suddenly, Last Summer
Directed by Joseph L Mankiewicz, 1959

Suspicion
Directed by Alfred Hitchcock, 1941

Sweet Smell Of Success
Directed by Alexander Mackendrick, 1957

The Talk Of The Town
Directed by George Stevens, 1942

That Touch Of Mink
Directed by Delbert Mann, 1962

Thelma & Louise
Directed by Ridley Scott, 1991

There's Something About Mary
Directed by Bobby and Peter Farrelly, 1998

The Thin Man
Directed by WS Van Dyke, 1934

The Thin Man Goes Home
Directed by Richard Thorpe, 1944

This Gun For Hire
Directed by Frank Tuttle, 1942

To Die For
Directed by Gus Van Sant, 1995

Tootsie
Directed by Sydney Pollack, 1982

Torch Song Trilogy
Directed by Paul Bogart, 1988

A Touch Of Class
Directed by Melvin Frank, 1973

The Two Mrs Carrolls
Directed by Peter Godfrey, 1947

Used People
Directed by Beeban Kidron, 1992

Victor/Victoria
Directed by Blake Edwards, 1982

War Of The Roses
Directed by Danny DeVito, 1989

We're No Angels
Directed by Michael Curtiz, 1955

Who's Afraid Of Virginia Woolf?
Directed by Mike Nichols, 1966

Wild Things
Directed by John McNaughton, 1998

The Witches Of Eastwick
Directed by George Miller, 1987

Witness For The Prosecution
Directed by Billy Wilder, 1957

Woman Of The Year
Directed by George Stevens, 1942

The Women
Directed by George Cukor, 1939

INDEX OF MOVIES

INDEX OF ACTORS